Written by Suzanna Hayes-Goldfinch
Designed by Chris Dalrymple

A Pillar Box Red Publication

©2016. Published by Pillar Box Red Publishing Ltd.

This is an independent publication. It is completely unofficial and unauthorised and, as such, has no connection with the artist or artists featured, or with any organisation or individual connected in any way whatsoever with the artist or artists featured.

Any quotes within this publication which are attributed to a celebrity, or celebrities, featured have been sourced from other publications, or from the internet, and, as such, are a matter of public record. They have not been given directly to the author by the celebrity, or celebrities, themselves.

Whilst every effort has been made to ensure the accuracy of information within this publication, the publisher shall have no liability to any person or entity with respect to any inaccuracy, misleading information, loss or damage caused directly or indirectly by the information contained within this book.

The views expressed are solely those of the author and do not reflect the opinions of Pillar Box Red Publishing Ltd. All rights reserved. Printed in the EU.

ISBN 978-1-907823-77-0

Images © Rex Features and Shutterstock.com

Contents

 8 Meet the Vlog Stars

 26 Puzzles
- True or False
- Which YouTuber Are You?
- Anagrams
- Spot the Difference

 10 Tips for Your Vlog

 28 Superwoman
30 Roman Atwood
32 Pointless Blog
34 Rhett and Link
36 Zoella

 12 Vlogging Quiz

 13 Vlogspace

 38 Other Vloggers Worth a Mention

 14 PewDiePie
16 Smosh
18 KSI
20 Rosanna Pansino
22 Michelle Phan

 40 Noobs in 2017

 24 Vlogger Pets

 42 Before the Fame

 44 Where do Vloggers Get Their Ideas?

 53 When Vloggers Unite

 45 How do YouYube Stars Choose Their Vlogging Alias?

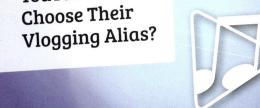 54 Music to Our Ears

 46 Time to Vlog

 56 Best Fashion Moments in Vlogging

 48 How Vloggers Make Their Money

 58 Puzzles
- Crossword
- Wordsearch

 50 The Most Outrageous Moments in Vlogging… Ever!

 60 Quiz Answers

 52 Celebrity Vloggers

 62 Where's Alfie?

Meet the Vlog Stars

Welcome to the wonderful world of vlogging, a place where a complete stranger can feel like your best friend by inviting you into their crazy, exciting, silly world. The vlogging universe is open to everyone; nobody is excluded. And that's why we love it!

We live in a digital age, where celebrities have to be accessible to be relevant. Thanks to YouTube, our favourite vloggers are easily contactable and relatable, and that's why millions of us are tuning in to watch their latest videos.

Enjoy this Vlogger's Annual, a fun-filled book jam-packed with all of your favourite video stars. Get the lowdown on some of the top vloggers, and discover new YouTubers to entertain you in 2017. You can also test your vlogger knowledge with some fun quizzes, and pick up some tips to improve your own vlogs, so that maybe one day, you can be a vlog superstar too...!

Vlogging in Numbers

8 million: The number of views a day when the site officially opened in 2005.

1.65 million: The number of dollars that Google paid to buy YouTube in 2006.

554,000: The number of sq feet in the new YouTube office headquarters.

76: The number of different languages you can watch YouTube in.

9: The number of April Fools' Day pranks YouTube has pulled on its users.

11: The number of years that YouTube has been running.

Where It All Began

Once upon a time, three PayPal employees had a plan for a revolutionary new website. Chad Hurley, Steve Chen and Jawed Karim wanted to create a platform for users to share their videos, and in 2005 a beta version was released to the public.

The very first video was of Jawed Karim at the zoo, and you can still view it today if you look for "Me at the zoo". When the site first officially launched it was receiving eight million views a day, and this figure has risen significantly to over four billion.

As well as giving us a plethora of vlogging stars to watch, YouTube is also responsible for launching the careers of many an aspiring pop star, including Justin Bieber, The Weeknd and 5 Seconds of Summer. It is safe to say that YouTube has well and truly become a part of modern life.

Internet Pranksters

It's not just the vloggers who are pulling pranks on each other; every April Fools' Day, YouTube has managed to trick us with some pretty hilarious gags. In 2008, every video on the home page linked to a Rick Astley song, and so started the craze of 'rick-rolling'. In 2012, YouTube convinced users that they could buy a DVD boxset of every video ever uploaded, and in 2016 viewers were treated to 360-degree views and Snoop Dogg commentary, known as Snoopa Vision. Those tricksters...!

Tips for Your Vlog

✓ If you are thinking of starting your own vlog, or maybe you are looking for ways to jazz up the one you already have, take some advice from the experts.

Zoella
"As long as you are putting in the effort and filming things that you love, and that your audience are interested in, you'll do well."
(The Guardian, 2014)

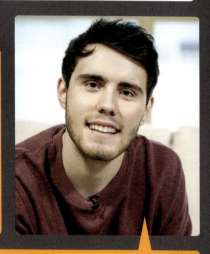

Anthony Padilla (Smosh)
"In reality, creating stuff online is about creating something that you enjoy, that your friends are going to enjoy, that you could really put your heart into and people that watch it will really see that and gravitate towards that."
(Dolly.com, 2015)

Alfie Deyes
"You should upload regularly. I'm saying maybe like twice a week, or something like that, just because if you create a schedule and people know when your videos are going up, then they just get into a routine."
(MTV, 2015)

Tanya Burr
"Make sure you are on social media. Be active online and make sure you are talked about. A simple Tweet or Facebook post can reach a large audience in seconds! It's a great way to build your brand and get your name recognised."
(The Express, 2014)

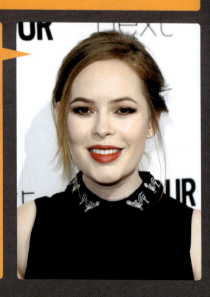

Superwoman

"Accept that no matter what you do or say, people will say mean things. Develop thick skin! And if comments do get to you, I find eating buttery popcorn helps."

(Vogue, 2015)

Tyler Oakley

"Start today, as soon as you want to start; start, because a year from now you'll wish you started a year ago."

(Radio Times, 2015)

Niomi Smart

"I think it's important to have your own niche topic that people know you for and this in turn will establish a clear brand identity."

(Asos.com, 2016)

Oli White

"Do it because you love it, don't do it because you want to get some money or become famous because that's not the right way to go."

(Ten Eighty Magazine, 2015)

Allie Marie Evans

"Network, network, network. YouTube has become incredibly popular and chances are there are tons of other people just starting out who would love to collab with you. Come together with other creators of a similar size and help each other grow by introducing your existing fan base to your new online friends."

(Glamour Magazine, 2015)

Sprinkle of Glitter

"Either sit in front of a window when it's nice and sunny, or have some lights in front of your face, so that you are well lit."

(ITV, 2015)

Vlogging Quiz

How well do you know your video bloggers?

1 Which beauty vlog star is married to fellow YouTuber Jim Chapman?

a. Michelle Phan
b. Marzia Bisognin
c. Tanya Burr ✓
d. Lisa Eldridge

2 Which Brighton-based stunt vlogger has an alter ego named Margaret?

a. Troye Sivan   b. Marcus Butler
c. Joseph Garrett   d. Joe Sugg ✓

3 Which video star was on her way to becoming an interior designer before finding fame?

a. Zoe Sugg   b. Louise Pentland
c. Cherry Wallis   d. Lilly Singh

4 Which young vlogster counts Simon Cowell as a fan?

a. Jim Chapman
b. Joe Sugg ✓
c. Michelle Phan
d. Caspar Lee

5 Which energetic YouTube prankster grew up in South Africa before moving to London?

a. Caspar Lee ✓
b. Lisa Eldridge
c. Shane Dawson
d. Louis Cole

6 Which charming vlogging pioneer began his career aged just 16 years old?

a. Caspar Lee   b. Jim Chapman
c. Tom Cassell   d. Alfie Deyes ✓

7 Which Swedish gamer vlogger refers to his fans as "The Bro Army"?

a. Joseph Garrett   b. Troye Sivan
c. Louis Cole   d. PewDiePie ✓

8 Which vlogging couple has been transformed into a waxwork at Madame Tussauds?

a. Jim Chapman and Tanya Burr
b. PewDiePie and Marzia Bisognin
c. Alfie Deyes and Zoe Sugg ✓
d. Niomi Smart and Marcus Butler

Answers on page 60

Vlogspace

In August 2016 Google opened YouTube Space at their offices in King's Cross, London. Once you get over 10,000 subscribers you can get free access to the Space's professional studio facilities. All you need to take your vlogging career to the next level. Cool huh?

YouTube creators pose for a group photo inside the YouTube Space.

The red carpet at the YouTube Space launch event.

PewDiePie

Who is PewDiePie?

If you haven't already heard of PewDiePie, real name Felix Arvid Ulf Kjellberg, then where on earth have you been? This YouTuber is one of the most popular vloggers on planet Earth right now, regularly topping the charts for the amount of subscribers he has and the money he earns. He infuriated his parents by dropping out of university in order to focus on his vlogging career, subsidising his computer game habit by working on a hot dog stand for a while, but it seems like a move that has more than paid off.

Factfile:

Birthday: October 24th, 1989.
Home: Brighton, UK.
Family: Felix lives with his vlogger girlfriend, Marzia Bisognin, and their two pug dogs.
Most subscribed video: A Funny Montage – 73 million views.
Awards: Shorty Award for Best in Gaming, 2013; Teen Choice Award for Choice Web Star: Gaming, 2014; Shorty Award for Gamer, 2015.

PewDiePie Channel

Felix began vlogging back in 2010, filming himself playing games under the moniker Pewdie. However, he soon forgot the password to that YouTube account, and so had to create a fresh one, which is the PewDiePie account we know and love today. As well as Let's Play videos that are filled with Felix's goofy personality and scattered with curse words, he also uploads snippets of his daily life on a video series called 'Fridays with Pewdie'. By February 2013, he had become the most subscribed user on YouTube, a title he has held ever since.

Quote about being the biggest earner on YouTube:

"It seems like the whole world cares more about how much money I make than I do myself." (www.YouTube.com)

Did you know?

PewDiePie has a Taylor Swift obsession. He hounded her on Twitter for almost two years until she finally caved in and followed him back. When Swift's Twitter was hacked, private messages between the two were unveiled, proving their internet friendship.

Routine:

Felix likes to record his videos in the afternoon, editing them the following morning before uploading. He uploads almost every day, sometimes twice, so there is always new content for his fans.

Smosh

Who are Smosh?

Smosh are a comedy duo made up of two friends, Ian Andrew Hecox and Anthony Padilla. The boys met in sixth grade at their Californian school, when they were paired together on a science project, and they have been inseparable ever since. Some messing around with a webcam in their bedrooms soon led to viral success and then their place as one of the most successful YouTube channels in the world. There are ten separate Smosh channels, although not all have scheduled content, and some are run by fans rather than the boys themselves. They have also released songs that have hit the UK and US music charts.

Factfile:

Birthdays: Ian – November 30th, 1987; Anthony – September 16th, 1987.
Home: California, USA.
Family: Both Ian's parents have popped up in Smosh vlogs. He is currently in a relationship with Pamela Horton. Anthony lives alone with his pet cat, Pip, although he is dating Miel Bredouw.
Most subscribed video: Beef 'n Go – 102 million views.
Awards: Webby Award for Gaming, 2016; Short Award for YouTube Star of the Year, 2015; Streamy Award for Best Gaming Channel, 2014; Social Star Award for United States Social Media Star, 2013; YouTube Award for Comedy, 2006.

Smosh Channel

Padilla began making videos back in 2003, on social media site Newgrounds. He was joined by Hecox in 2005, which is when they created their first YouTube channel. By May 2006 it was the most subscribed channel, an accolade they have since lost to PewDiePie.

Originally, the channel saw the friends making animated videos and sketches of them lip-syncing along to popular children's programmes. As their popularity grew, they started to make a series of short skits, including 'Pokemon in Real Life' and 'Ian is Bored'. Three new channels were created in 2012, which saw Smosh diversify into Spanish, cartoons and gaming. This year they released a sitcom called 'Part-Timers' which is very loosely based on Hecox's life. And they have even made a Hollywood film!

Quote about the Smosh movie:

"Doing new things like this definitely keeps us from getting bored, y'know. We were doing this for almost ten years now, so throwing in fun new things for us to do is definitely welcome."
(www.YouTube.com)

Did you know?

Anthony has some serious web skills. As well as knowing how to make and edit YouTube videos, he is able to create fully functional websites. He used to sell his website-making services for $100.

Routine:

The boys upload to their main Smosh channel three times a week. Smosh Games receives seven uploads a week, while the Smosh 2nd Channel is twice a week. They have other channels that they also regularly upload videos to. These boys certainly like to keep busy!

> Follow Smosh:
> www.smosh.com
> YouTube: /Smosh
> Twitter: @smosh
> Instagram: @smosh
> Facebook: /Smosh

Spotlight on

KSI

Who is KSI?

Olajide Olatunji is the man behind KSI. The comedian, rapper, actor and prankster has built up quite a name for himself in the YouTube community, thanks to his funny sketches and fun sporting challenges. He is a vlog veteran, having started out with the channel JideJunior in 2008. Many of his videos feature him rapping original songs with other people, and he has even had limited success in the UK charts. His talents have also extended to writing, and he has released a book entitled, *KSI: I Am a Bellend*.

Factfile:

Birthday: June 19th, 1993.
Home: Watford, UK.
Family: He has a brother called Oladeji, who can also be found on YouTube under the name ComedyShortsGamer.
Most viewed video: KSI – Lamborghini ft. P Money - 43 million views.
Awards: NME Award for Vlogger of the Year, 2016.

KSI Channel

The vlog began back in 2009, and originally mainly consisted of FIFA gameplay videos. He soon branched out into other games such as Grand Theft Auto and Mortal Kombat, and now each upload focuses on his other interests, including rapping, pranking and fun sketches. He often teams up with his friends, Ethan Payne, Simon Minter, Josh Bradley, Tobi Brown, Vikram Barn and Harry Lewis; together they call themselves the Sidemen. For every fan he has, KSI has just as many critics, due to his obscene language, and sometimes inappropriate behaviour. He is definitely a character that viewers either love or hate.

Quote about his success:

"I'm now a brand. Like, KSI is a brand. It's crazy that it all came from me sitting in my bedroom just making a few FIFA videos." (www.vice.com)

Did you know?

KSI has a Guinness World Record for Most Goals Scored Against a Computer. He was awarded the accolade in 2013 with 190 goals.

Routine:

Olajide has been known to stay awake all night editing and filming for his channel, so he often uploads videos in the morning. He has no strict routine, instead working whenever he feels inspired.

Rosanna Pansino

Who is Rosanna Pansino?

Rosanna Pansino has built her career in the kitchen, filming baking videos which showcase her infectious, bubbly personality. Her YouTube series, 'Nerdy Nummies', has been a big hit, placing her firmly amongst the best paid YouTubers in the world. She has worked since she was 15 years old, and, adhering to advice her father gave her, she has always saved 10% of everything she has ever earned. It was these savings she used to launch her vlogging career, a move that has certainly paid off!

Factfile:

Birthday: June 8th, 1985.
Home: California, USA.
Family: Rosanna's family are all part of her YouTube team. Her mum, dad, and sister Molly all help out. She also has a French bulldog named Cookie.
Most subscribed video: How to Make a Frozen Princess Cake – 126 million views.
Awards: Shorty Award for Best in Food, 2013.

Nerdy Nummies

It was back in 2011 when Rosanna posted her first video on YouTube. It was a video of her volunteering on Earth Day, closely followed up by a video of her baking a Super Mario birthday cake. The tools she used were amateur and poor quality, but when she began to take her vlogging career more seriously, she invested in much better equipment. She now makes $2.5million a year with her baking videos, and has also released a cookbook called *The Nerdy Nummies Cookbook: Sweet Treats for the Geek in All of Us*. She often collaborates with other YouTube stars, including Bethany Mota, Grace Helbig and Smosh, creating baking delights for them.

Quote on the inspiration behind her channel:

"I started my geeky baking show because I wanted to combine two of my favourite things: I love baking as a hobby, and I love gaming." (www.YouTube.com)

Did you know?

Rosanna gave up an acting career to make her name on YouTube. She has appeared on episodes of *Glee* and *CSI*.

Routine:

Rosanna uploads videos every Tuesday, and has not missed one week since she started. It takes a whole week to prepare for the video, and then three hours to make and edit. She usually wakes at 6am and does a workout before spending up to 18 hours a day in the kitchen!

▶ Follow Rosanna Pansino:
www.rosannapansino.com
YouTube: /RosannaPansino
Twitter: @RosannaPansino
Instagram: @rosannapansino
Facebook: /rosannapansino

Michelle Phan

Who is Michelle Phan?

Michelle Phan is a highly regarded make-up artist who has made her name through make-up tutorials on YouTube. Not only does she have an army of fans who hang on her every make-up brush, but she has also spent time working as a representative for Lancôme and has even co-released a number of make-up ranges. More recently, she has diversified her interests, and created a talent network, written a book and launched Shift Music Group. She is truly an unstoppable entrepreneur.

Factfile:

Birthday: April 11th, 1987.
Home: Massachusetts, USA.
Family: The middle child, Michelle has an older brother and younger sister. She has been with her boyfriend, Dominique Capraro since 2010.
Most subscribed video: Barbie Transformation – 65 million views.
Awards: Streamy Award for Inspiration Icon, 2014; Shorty Award for Best YouTube Guru, 2014.

Michelle Phan Channel

Michelle posted her first YouTube video in May 2007, but she had already been blogging and vlogging via Xanga for two years by then. She aimed to emulate the production style of Bob Ross, enjoying his style of narration and voiceover. Her big break came when two of her videos were featured on BuzzFeed, which instantly helped them go viral and helped her subscriber count to grow. She now has over seven million subscribers who love her quirky personality and natural creative talent, and she was the first woman to reach one billion views.

As well as producing incredible make-up tutorials, Michelle also offers advice to her viewers. From how to reduce acne and combat cyber bullying, to business advice and how to handle rejection, she tackles issues that her fans will relate to and can hopefully learn from.

Quote on the key to success:

"You have to have a very striking idea, an idea that no one has done before yet, and you might think 'oh well everyone's done it' but, no, no, no, no, there's so many other untouched ideas, and everyone has a unique fingerprint." (www.YouTube.com)

Did you know?

Michelle Phan's story is a true rags-to-riches tale. Growing up, her family survived on food stamps, but now her empire is worth almost $100 million. Now she wants to help out any budding entrepreneurs so that others can emulate her success.

Routine:

Michelle uploads videos to her YouTube account and website daily. However, the subject matter seems to be what feels right at the time.

Follow Michelle Phan:
www.michellephan.com
YouTube: /MichellePhan
Twitter: @MichellePhan
Instagram: @michellephan
Facebook: /MichellePhanOfficial

Vlogger Pets

Our favourite vloggers' furry companions often make appearances in their videos. Their four-legged friends are almost as famous as their owners, so we think they deserve their own profiles in this book. Meet the pets of YouTube!

Mr Bear
The frisky feline belongs to model vlogger, Ruth Crilly. Mr Bear is a British Shorthair cat who moved in with Ruth back in 2012. With those gorgeous big paws, perfectly straight whiskers and strawberry blonde complexion, he was just made for video fame.

Reggie
Essie Button rescued Reggie the Greyhound back in 2013. After being initially nervous of cars, stairs and the camera, he has made a number of reluctant appearances on screen, and Essie's followers are always keen to know how he is.

Edgar
Little Edgar the Pug belongs to internet sensation PewDiePie. He first introduced the flat-nosed pup to the world in 2013, when he arranged a meeting between Edgar and his two other dogs. The petite black Pug has become known for his slightly nervous behaviour and tendency to chew computer wires.

Pippin and Percy
These two little balls of fluff belong to superstar Zoella. She first took the guinea pigs back to her home in 2014 where she treated us to lots of videos of the rodents and shopping hauls in their honour.

Pip
The Savannah cat belongs to Anthony from Smosh. The playful, camera-loving kitty is unusual because she enjoys being in water. She was also the inspiration for the expression "pipacity" which the Smosh boys use when they feel Pip has hogged too much air time.

Martha
Martha became a part of Tanya Burr and Jim Chapman's family in the summer of 2015. The miniature Dachshund caused controversy when it jumped into Tanya's bath, with many viewers worried about the effect it would have on the pup's skin. Thankfully, little Martha seems fine and the camera loves her!

Rocket and Zula
These two pesky kittens came into the life of Sprinkle of Glitter star, Louise Pentland, in 2014. Louise regularly refers to herself as a crazy cat lady, but the cute cats rarely play by the rules for the camera. If Louise wants to talk about the cats, they scarper, but if she is talking about something else, they will often gate-crash the vlog.

Goose
Grace Helbig's pup is a mix between a Bulldog and a Boston Terrier. The cuddly dog loves the spotlight, and as well as making several cameos in Grace's videos, she also has her own social media following, with accounts on Twitter and Instagram.

Puzzles

True or False:

1. PewDiePie met his girlfriend at a fan event............ ✓
2. Rhett and Link are brothers.................................. ✗
3. Rosanna Pansino has a dog called Cookie............ ✗
4. Roman Atwood once filled his house with balls...... ✓
5. Alfie Deyes lives in California................................ ✗

Which YouTuber Are You?

1. When people come to visit, how do you entertain them?
a. Bake a cake
b. Involve them in an elaborate prank *(circled)*
c. Play computer games
d. Do their make-up

2. When you are feeling low, how do you cheer yourself up?
a. Eat cake
b. Plan your next prank *(circled)*
c. Buy a new computer game
d. Organise your make-up bag

3. What's your ideal date?
a. A fun trip to the local café for coffee and cake *(circled)*
b. Pranking people in the park
c. A computer game convention
d. A club where I can show off my sick make-up skills

4. What is your backup plan if vlogging doesn't work?
a. Cake-making, obviously
b. Acting – my poker face is too good to waste *(circled)*
c. Something high-pressure. I almost completed my degree in Industrial Economics you know!
d. A freelance make-up artist

Most like Roman Atwood (Mostly Bs)

Anagrams
See if you can figure out who these well-known Vloggers are:

1. Cruel Bum Star — *Marcus Butler*
2. Aces Repel — *Caspar Lee*
3. ~~Early hands~~ — *Alfie Deyes*
4. A Spoiled Tunnel — *Louise Pentland*
5. Jug Goes — *Joe Sugg*
6. Hello Dawn — *Dan Howell*
7. Arty Urban — *Tanya Burr*
8. ~~The Maanbot~~ — *Bethany Mota*

Answers on page 60

Spot the Difference

There are ten differences between the two pictures – can you spot them all?

Answers on page 60

Spotlight on Superwoman

Who is Superwoman?

Lilly Singh is a comedian/vlogger who entered the world of YouTube in 2010. She has had a well-documented battle with depression, and uses vlogging as a way to deal with her feelings. Her Punjabi background often features in her videos, as she makes sure to recognise her beginnings now that she is in the top ten list of Forbes' highest earning YouTubers. Her career has enabled her to rap on songs, make cameos on a couple of movies and even undertake a world tour.

Factfile:

Birthday: September 26th, 1988.
Home: California, USA.
Family: Her parents are Sukhwinder Singh and Malwinder Singh, and she has an older sister called Tina.
Most subscribed video: How Girls Get Ready – 19 million.
Awards: MTV Fandom Award for Social Superstar of the Year, 2015; Streamy Award for First Person, 2015.

IISuperwomanII

Lilly currently has two channels that she regularly posts to. IISuperwomanII is her most popular and original channel where she posts funny sketches and rants. Her second channel is Superwomanvlogs, which is where she uploads videos of her day to day life. Her YouTube career began back in 2010, when she uploaded her first vlog, which was actually a serious depiction of How to Tie a Side Turla Bhangra Pagh. She now has over nine million subscribers who love her comedic vlogs.

Quote on her life goal:

"To be happy. I've experienced way too much in my life to say anything else. It doesn't matter what job, what academic stuff happens, what relationship stuff; I just want to be happy." (www.flare.com)

Did you know?

Lilly is very well educated. She has a degree in Psychology from York University, but took her career in a completely different direction when she became popular on YouTube.

Routine:

Lilly uploads videos to her main account every Monday and Thursday. She uploads daily vlogs to her second channel.

▶ Follow IISuperwomanII:
www.superwomanfandom.weebly.com
YouTube: /IISuperwomanII
Twitter: @IISuperwomanII
Instagram: @iisuperwomanii
Facebook: /IISuperwomanII

Roman Atwood

Who is Roman Atwood?

Before his YouTube career began, Roman Atwood worked in his family's rope business. Now he is one of the top YouTube hidden camera pranksters in the world, with nine million subscribers. He has always loved creating videos, and has been filming and producing them since high school, even creating a series of DVDs called Nerd Herd. Along with some of his vlogger peers, he released a film in 2016 called *Natural Born Pranksters*. He has also worked on commercials.

Factfile:

Birthday: May 28th, 1983.
Home: Ohio, USA.
Family: Roman chooses to live in Ohio to stay close to his extended family. He lives with his girlfriend Brittney, two sons, Noah and Kane, and dog, Zeus, who all regularly appear in his videos.
Most subscribed video: Anniversary Prank Backfires – 81 million.
Awards: Streamy Award for best brand campaign with the plastic ball prank, 2015; Shorty Award for YouTube Comedian, 2016.

Roman Atwood Channels

Although Roman Atwood is mostly known for his outrageous and sometimes controversial pranks, he actually spends a lot of time simply vlogging his daily life with his family. These videos are on a separate channel called Roman Atwood Vlogs, and they allow fans to see inside Roman's beautiful home and get to know his girlfriend, sons and dog. However, it is his pranks on his main channel that tend to gather the most attention. His plastic ball prank, in which he filled his entire house with plastic balls, was noticed by the makers of the Nissan GTR, who used the video in their commercial.

Quote on how he got started:

"It was just a hobby. I've done this since I was a little kid. I've produced full-length DVDs on my own that I used to go out on Warped Tour, and try to hustle these kids to buy, and YouTube was just a place for me to host the content." (www.roverradio.com)

Did you know?

Roman Atwood was actually married before he met Brittney. He was just 18 years old when he married, and it ended in divorce. His oldest son came from this first marriage, and Roman has custody.

Routine:

Roman uploads to his RomanAtwoodVlogs channel almost daily. However, his main channel tends to be a monthly upload, presumably due to the time it takes to plan and organise the events.

Pointless Blog

Who is behind the Pointless Blog?

Alfie Deyes is a charming, lovable character who now has three YouTube channels. Pointless Blog is his main channel, but he also owns PointlessBlogGames and PointlessBlogVlogs. Like his girlfriend, Zoella, he has ventured into the world of publishing, and has released three books. His positive attitude towards life and silly, boyish pranks have earned him five million subscribers.

Factfile:

Birthday: September 17th, 1993.
Home: Brighton, UK.
Family: Alfie lives with his girlfriend, Zoella, who is also a vlogger. His sister, Poppy Deyes, is also an aspiring YouTube star.
Most subscribed video: Ariana Grande Does My Makeup – 14 million views.
Awards: Alfie has been nominated for a Teen Choice Award in 2014, a Nickelodeon Kids Choice Award in 2015, and a BBC Radio 1 Teen Award in 2015, but is sadly yet to win any.

PointlessBlog

The Pointless Blog began in 2009, and mostly features Alfie and his friends trying out silly challenges or making funny sketches. Alfie is just as popular in YouTube land as he is with his subscribers, so he is able to do a lot of collaborations, even pulling in superstars like Ariana Grande to help him. PointlessBlogGames features Alfie playing computer games, while PointlessBlogVlogs features Alfie in his day-to-day life. Unsurprisingly, we see a lot of Zoe Suggs, his girlfriend, in his videos.

Quote on career goals:

"The main thing I've learned and that I really try to tell my audience, my family, and my friends is that there is really no point in life doing a job that doesn't make you happy. The main message I try to convey is to do what makes you happy, because you never know what's going to happen." (www.huffingtonpost.com)

Did you know?

Alfie was 15 when he uploaded his first ever video to YouTube – proof that you don't need to wait until you are an adult to start achieving your dreams.

Routine:

Unlike other YouTubers, Alfie is adamant that he does not stick to a filming schedule, instead filming as and when he feels the need. Usually, however, he will upload a vlog the day after he has filmed it.

Follow Pointless Blog:
www.pointlessblogshop.com
YouTube: /PointlessBlogTV
Twitter: @PointlessBlog
Instagram: @pointlessblog
Facebook: /AlfieDeyes

Rhett and Link

Who are Rhett and Link?

You may know Rhett James Mclaughlin and Charles Lincoln Neal III better as the Good Mythical Morning Duo. They refer to themselves as 'internetainers' and they have four channels that they regularly upload to. Having been best friends since their very first year at school, they even went to university together and completed engineering degrees. They now have almost 11 million subscribers on their second channel, and have earned themselves a place on the Forbes list of Richest Vloggers.

Factfile:

Birthdays: October 11th, 1977 (Rhett); June 1st, 1978 (Link).
Home: California, USA.
Family: Rhett is married to Jessie, and they have two sons together. Link is married to Christy, and they have three children.
Most subscribed video: Eating a Scorpion – Bug War Challenge – 23 million views.
Awards: Webby Award for Best Editing, 2011; IAWTV Award for Best Variety Series, 2013; LA Web Award for Funniest YouTube Video, 2013; Webby Award for Comedy Individual Short or Episode, 2014; Webby Awards for Viral (Branded), Viral Channel, and First Person, 2015; Streamy Award for Non-Fiction, 2015; Shorty Awards for Best Podcast and Best Web Series, 2016; Webby Award for Best Web Personality, 2016.

Good Mythical Morning

As the boys' second channel (the first is called Rhett & Link), Good Mythical Morning is even more popular than the first. The very first upload was back in 2008, entitled The Bloody Door. Since then, they have continued to upload silly sketches on the channel they call their Morning Talk Show. Their music videos, commercials and other sketches are usually uploaded to the Rhett & Link channel. If you like the sound of videos such as '8 Weirdest Things Sent by Mail' and 'Breaking Dumb Laws', then Good Mythical Morning is definitely a channel you should be watching.

Quote on when they decided they would work together:

"Early on we kind of decided we were going to work together. In fact, we were in middle school – middle school or early high school – when we did that blood oath thing."
(www.newmediarockstars.com)

Did you know?

Rhett and Link appeared in the video for LMFAO's Sorry for Party Rocking. If you hadn't noticed them, it's because they are in the zebra costume, shuffling on the dance floor!

Routine:

Rhett and Link upload a video to Good Mythical Morning daily. The content for their other channels is not as routinely uploaded, so fans are encouraged to check back often so they don't miss new videos.

Spotlight on

Zoella

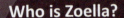

Who is Zoella?

The quirky, excitable Zoe Elizabeth Sugg is a fashion and beauty vlogger who is famous for her videos of shopping hauls and favourite products. Like many of her fellow YouTubers, she has diversified from vlogging to become a writer, with her debut book having the highest first week sales of a first-time author since they started keeping records in 1998. She is also an ambassador for the National Citizen Service, and for Mind, the mental health charity, and has a range of make-up which sells in Superdrug. She is one of the most instantly recognisable vloggers.

Factfile:

Birthday: March 28th, 1990.
Home: Brighton, UK.
Family: Zoella lives with her boyfriend, Alfie Deyes, who is also a vlogger. Her brother, Joe Sugg, is known as Thatcher Joe to the YouTube community.
Most subscribed video: 7 Second Challenge with Miranda Sings – 18.5 million views.
Awards: Cosmopolitan Blog Award for Best Established Beauty Blog, 2011; Cosmopolitan Blog Award for Best Beauty Vlogger, 2012; Nickelodeon Kids Choice Award for UK Favourite Vlogger, 2014; Teen Choice Award for Choice Webstar Fashion/Beauty, 2014 and 2015.

Zoella

The Zoella channel began back in 2009 as a blog when Zoella was working as an apprentice for an interior design firm. By the end of the year it had become a YouTube vlog and had over a thousand subscribers. Now she can boast almost 11 million subscribers, and counts a large number of YouTube vloggers as her friends, which enables her to collaborate with them often. She has another channel called MoreZoella, which charts her day-to-day life.

Quote on fame:

"It's not something I could have prepared myself for. Every day I am still coming to terms with this, it's not gone to my head." (www.vogue.co.uk)

Did you know?

Zoella and her boyfriend Alfie were the first YouTubers to be immortalised in wax form at Madame Tussauds. The moment the figures were unveiled showed just how huge the vlogging phenomenon had become.

Routine:

Zoe uploads to her main channel weekly, usually on a Sunday. Her second channel sees daily uploads.

▶ Follow Zoella:
www.zoella.co.uk
YouTube: /zoella280390
Twitter: @Zoella
Instagram: @zoella
Facebook: /zoe.zoella

Other Vloggers Worth a Mention

Louise Pentland
Sprinkle of Glitter – vlogging since 2010, Louise videos her shopping hauls, beauty regime and inspirational advice. Her most popular video is Louise or Zoe, with 3 million views.

Jim Chapman
Jim started out in 2009 by vlogging about men's fashion and grooming. Now he videos himself doing all sorts of things. His most popular video is Joe Sugg Waxed My Armpits, with almost 4 million views.

Phil Lester
Amazing Phil: Phil vlogs less regularly than most YouTubers, but our journey through his fun and silly life is always worth the wait. His most popular video is Phil is Not on Fire 6 with almost 8 million views.

Charlie McDonnell
Charlieissocoollike: The first vlogger in the UK to hit the 1 million subscribers mark, Charlie's vlogs include sketches, songs, short films and science. His most popular video is My American Accent with 10 million views.

Tanya Burr

The make-up artist uploads celebrity beauty tutorials, baking videos and shopping hauls. Her most popular video is Tanya Burr & Zoella 3 Minute Make-up Challenge with 4.5 million views.

Marcus Butler

Pranks, sketches, advice and videos on his views on life make up Marcus' YouTube channel. His most popular video is Impressions with Helium with 9 million views.

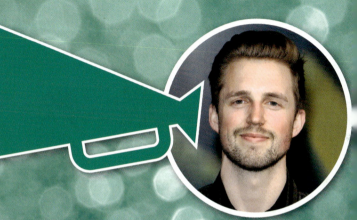

Caspar Lee

Caspar uploads pranks, challenges and general vlogs of his day-to-day life on his YouTube channel. His most popular video is Girlfriend Pranks my Roommate with 18 million views.

Dan Howell

Danisnotonfire: Vlogs based on his awkwardness make up this quirky YouTube channel. Watch sketches, pranks and videos of his daily life. His most popular video is The Photo Booth Challenge with 13 million views.

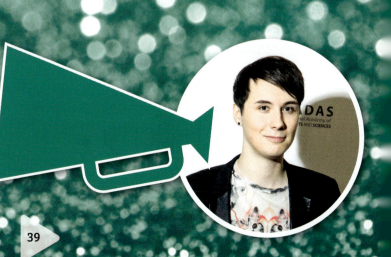

Noobs in 2017

2017!

Our favourite YouTube stars might have millions of followers now, but it took them years of hard work and self-belief to get to the stage they are at today. Who has been quietly plodding away in the background hoping to benefit from some of the same stardom? Here are the names to look out for in 2017. Believe us, they are going to be big!

Kota Jones
Kota is an author who vlogs about how she writes. Her vlog is brand new and ideal for aspiring novelists or those that love to read!

Kathleen Lights
Kathleen is a beauty vlogger who has been a member of YouTube since 2013. Her channel has recently been gathering a lot more attention, which is undoubtedly due to her amazing make-up tutorials.

Cupcake Jemma

Watch Jemma make incredible cakes for her London-based shop. This is one vlog that will leave you hungry for more!

Mathew Nooch

A newbie to the world of gaming vlogs, Matthew is enthusiastic, fun and sure to capture your attention with his Let's Play videos.

KidPOV

This hilarious YouTuber is already friends with some of the biggest vlogger names, and he has clearly picked up some tips. His funny rants, drag make-up tutorials and light-hearted chatter will have you questioning everything in life that you consider 'normal'.

Evan Edinger Travel

With the personality of your favourite YouTubers but in much more interesting locations, Evan is a must watch vlogger for 2017.

Before The Fame

What did the world's most prolific YouTube stars do before they were able to make a living from vlogging?

Zoella

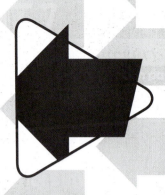

This perky YouTube princess was an apprentice for an interior designer when she started videoing her life. When she was made redundant she took a job at New Look, before her vlogging career took off and she was able to concentrate on YouTubing full time.

Danisnotonfire

Daniel Howell dropped out of his law degree at the University of Manchester in order to pursue fame and fortune through the internet. Somehow we just can't imagine life would have been as fun for Dan if he had gone through with his plans of becoming a lawyer.

Amazing Phil

Dan's best friend, Phil Lester, actually finished his studies before becoming YouTube famous. He is the proud owner of a degree in English Language and Linguistics, and a Masters in Video Production. This boy is more than just a pretty face!

Sprinkle of Glitter

Louise Pentland's vlogging career began when she started writing a blog entitled Sprinkle of Glitter. The blog was a hobby, which she wrote in her spare time while working in various office jobs. Prior to this, she attended Liverpool John Moores University.

Daily Grace
The witty, funny Grace Helbig is a former semi-finalist of the Miss New Jersey beauty pageant. Her desire to perform was only made stronger through attendance at Ramapo's School of Contemporary Arts and the People's Improv Theatre in New York. As well as creating video blogs, Grace has also had a number of minor acting roles.

Tanya Burr
Tanya has always been a beauty fanatic, and before she started uploading make-up tutorials, she worked on a department store beauty counter. What a great way to build up experience before taking over the beauty vlogging world!

PewDiePie
Felix Arvid Ulf Kjellberg could have followed a very different career path, had he not dropped out of university to concentrate on his YouTube obsession. If he had completed his degree in Industrial Economics and Technology Management, we may never have heard of our vlogger superstar!

Roman Atwood
This YouTube prankster may be all fun and frivolity now, but before he began vlogging he had a very boring job working in the family rope business, Atwood Rope. However, filming and producing was his hobby, and he was soon able to leave the rope industry to focus on making hilarious videos.

StampyLongNose
Joseph Garratt worked as a barman before giving it all up to play computer games for a living. His initial intention was to become a games journalist, after studying video production at university. After creating a few vlogs aimed at an older audience, he soon realised that his biggest fans were children, and he altered his content accordingly, hence the birth of StampyCat!

Superwoman
Lilly Singh began making YouTube videos as soon as she left university. She gained her degree in Psychology at York University, and began vlogging as a way to deal with her depression. And the rest is history!

Where do Vloggers Get Their Ideas?

Most vloggers start out by videoing themselves doing things that they love, so the ideas tend to flow naturally. However, as they become more successful, and pressure builds on them to provide more and more content, they often have to plan ahead a little. So how do they choose the subject of the day?

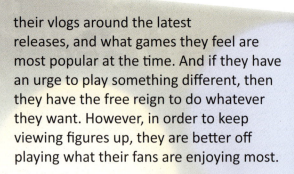

Often, veteran vloggers are paid to include goods provided by a company. While this makes it easier to come up with an idea for that video blog, the products must always be relevant to the vlogger, or the link will come across forced and insincere. Make-up and fashion vloggers, such as Zoella and Tanya Burr, often find themselves endorsing affiliate items.

Other vloggers prefer to have a rant of the day. Nigahiga is a pro at simply turning the camera on, and then proceeding to vent his frustrations on certain topics. This can often be fun and entertaining, but vloggers must always be careful not to become controversial or offensive.

Computer game vloggers such as PewDiePie and Dan DTM can schedule their vlogs around the latest releases, and what games they feel are most popular at the time. And if they have an urge to play something different, then they have the free reign to do whatever they want. However, in order to keep viewing figures up, they are better off playing what their fans are enjoying most.

And of course, it is the fans that matter when it comes to vlogging. Without viewers and subscribers, the vloggers would be as ordinary as you and me. So fan requests and suggestions play a big part in what the YouTubers decide to film. Never be afraid to make suggestions in the comments section of YouTube, as it gives the vloggers fresh ideas to work with.

How do YouTube Stars Choose Their Vlogging Alias?

Some vloggers upload videos under their own name, for example, Michelle Phan or Tanya Burr. Others try to be more inventive with their vlogging alias. But what makes a good name?

The name Good Mythical Morning comes from the boys' schooldays, when they were both kept in at lunchtime for drawing on the tables. It was their first meeting, and they sat together and drew mythical creatures. The memory is clearly one they have both treasured, as it was over 30 years ago!

Smosh chose their name after a slip of the tongue had them both in stitches. One of their friends accidentally said "smosh pit" instead of "mosh pit", and so the name was born.

Thatcher Joe has a fairly simple reasoning behind his YouTube handle. When he first started vlogging he was working as an apprentice for his thatcher uncle. Hence his thatcher name!

The reasoning behind the name VSauce was that Michael Stevens wanted a name that meant absolutely nothing. This ensured he could make whatever videos he fancied, without having to feel constrained by a theme.

There are no rules as to what you name your vlog, although it pays to bear in mind who your audience will be. And keep it clean to stay the right side of the YouTube censors!

Time to Vlog

Vlogging

Plan

So you've decided to take the plunge and create your first vlog? That's great! First of all, ensure that you have permission of a parent or guardian if you are under 18, as it will save any arguments later on!

And then you need a plan. While some seasoned vloggers are able to turn on the camera, chat away about nothing, and then get 500,000 hits, this is not going to happen to you (probably)! It takes a bit of experience to feel confident talking to a camera; with no immediate feedback it can be difficult to know if what you are saying is interesting to other people. And most YouTubers actually film a lot of footage which they edit down into videos that are only a few minutes long, to ensure they cut out anything boring. So it pays to plan, as it will reduce the amount of editing necessary. It will also stop you talking off subject and your viewers are less likely to lose interest.

Before you even start rolling the camera, you need to come up with a name and a purpose for your vlog. While the theme doesn't have to be completely rigid, having a specialist subject does help you attract the right kind of fans.

Permission

Theme

For example, Zoella is known for her shopping hauls; Tanya Burr is known for her make-up and baking; and PewDiePie is known for his gaming. That is not to say that they can't upload something else once in a while, but it will be their core subject that keeps viewers coming back for more.

Lighting

Account

And of course, you will need a YouTube account. This is another reason why you'll need mum and dad on side, since the YouTube terms and conditions form a contract which only those of legal age may accept. Once you have your account ready, a name and a theme, you'll want to consider your content.

What is the aim of your vlog? Do you want to film pranks, computer games or your hobbies? Do you have an important message to share with the world? Try to pick something unique, so that you are not just copying something that has already been done. For your very first video, it might pay to practise what you want to say a few times, to prevent stuttering and stumbling over your words. Have cue cards to practise with, so that you remember everything you want to say, and take some time to perfect your speaking speed. If you speak too quickly, your viewers won't be able to keep up with you; but speak too slow and you will bore them.

When it comes to the actual filming, lighting is very important. You could have the most expensive HD camera in the world, but if you are sitting under bad lighting, it won't matter. Sit in a well-lit area, and bring in some lamps to brighten it further. You could also try to sit by a window for some natural light. The aim is to make sure you have no shadows over your face, as this will be distracting to your viewers, and they won't be able to see you properly.

When you have uploaded your piece of art, share it with the world. Nobody will watch it if they don't know about it! Now is your time to shine! Good luck!

Share

47

How Vloggers Make Their Money

Whilst making, editing and producing videos may be fun, it is not a money-spinning career on its own. It takes hard work, dedication and a little bit of luck to be able to turn it into a sustainable job. This is how the big names made their fortunes.

Paid Ads
The advertisements that run before and alongside YouTube videos may be annoying, but they are the vlogger's premium source of income. Every time an advertisement is played, the team behind it pay the owner of the vlog a small amount of money. So the more viewers the vloggers attract, the more money they make. To set up adverts on your vlog, you will need to create a Google AdWords account. And you will need to work hard to generate a loyal audience.

Write a Book
Many vloggers have supplemented their earnings by writing a book. This is really only profitable for those who have an avid audience, eager to soak up everything the vlogger has to say. Big names like Zoella, Thatcher Joe, Sprinkle of Glitter and Miranda Sings have all written books about their vlogging interests. Zoella and Thatcher Joe even turned their hands to fiction, alhough Zoe has admitted to having a little help with this.

Product Placement

Product placement is sometimes just a fun way to get free things from advertisers, but many of the biggest YouTube stars charge a small fortune to let brands place items in their videos. Vloggers with a big enough audience are an extremely attractive proposition to brands who want their products advertised to a large number of their target demographic as quickly as possible. When someone like Caspar Lee is paid to talk about a certain product, it can sell out in minutes, and for that reason he is able to charge a hefty sum for a few seconds' work.

Create a Range of Beauty Products

Step into any Superdrug store, and you will see the faces of Zoe Sugg and Tanya Burr smiling back at you from the shelves. These side projects are extremely successful, since their viewers already trust them to impart beauty knowledge – it is part of the reason they watch them, after all.

Get discovered

For some, vlogging has opened the door to other platforms. Jim Chapman, for example, has been signed up by the modelling agency Models 1, and has dabbled in a bit of presenting. Of course, YouTube was responsible for launching the careers of Justin Bieber and Carly Rae Jepsen, and even played a part in the success of sports stars such as Havard Rugland.

While vlogging may not be a profitable business at the beginning, it certainly opens a lot of doors. A little bit of hard work, and you could soon see the cash rolling in!

The Most Outrageous Moments in Vlogging... Ever!

Those vloggers are a crazy bunch; never afraid to pull a funny prank or make a fool of themselves for our entertainment. But occasionally they take their jokes a bit too far, as you can see here!

MyPaleSkin

When beauty vlogger, Em Ford, also known as MyPaleSkin, uploaded a film called 'You Look Disgusting', she could never have anticipated the feedback she received. The film was about nasty comments she had received about her acne-prone skin, and it hit a nerve with many teens. Em uploaded the video at 9pm, and by the following morning she was being hounded by journalists wanting to talk to her about it. She has been praised by many as being inspirational, beautiful and a very talented make-up artist.

StampyLongNose

Ten year olds all over the world were outraged when Google terminated Joseph Garrett's YouTube account back in 2013. With no warning, and no explanation, Joseph was forced to turn to social media, and plead with his fans to campaign on his behalf. Hundreds of videos were uploaded to the site, begging for Stampy's reinstatement, and on Twitter, #savestampy started trending worldwide. Of course, this story had a happy ending, and StampyCat is back in action.

Nicole Arbour

In 2015, Nicole caused outrage by uploading a video named 'Dear Fat People'. The completely offensive, nasty and ignorant comments that she made were understandably upsetting to many. But despite the backlash, Nicole still went ahead and uploaded 'Dear Fat People 2', except this time she targeted the plus size model that was featured on the front of Sports Illustrated. Personally victimising a successful model was a step too far for many, and Nicole has firmly cemented her status as one of America's most hated people.

Roman Atwood

Roman has uploaded a few controversial pranks, but for some he went too far when he convinced his girlfriend that he had killed their son. Pretending to play fight with his child, who was dressed in a Spiderman outfit, he then threw him over the banister. Cue a crying, terrified girlfriend rushing to the rescue, only to find a mannequin on the floor. Despite the criticism he received for this vlog, he went on to upload a series of 'Killing my own Kid' videos.

BF vs GF

Okay, so this moment wasn't strictly 'outrageous', but it sure broke a lot of vloggers' hearts. When Jeana and Jesse poured their hearts out on their final video, and told the world that they were splitting, it was big, devastating news for the vlogging community. We can only hope that they come back again soon, whether as a couple or separately, so we can continue to enjoy their humorous pranks.

Celebrity Vloggers

So we've seen how a little time and effort can turn any vlogger into a celebrity, but what about those vloggers who were celebrities before they turned to YouTube?

More and more of our favourite mainstream stars are enjoying videoing themselves for our entertainment, with varying degrees of success. Let's take a look at some of the more noteworthy ones.

Tom Fletcher

The cute one from boy band McFly, Tom is now married with two children. And thanks to the wonderful world of YouTube, we know all about them! He also regularly blogs alongside his sister, Carrie Fletcher, under the pseudonym Its Way Past My Bedtime.

Charlotte Crosby

The *Geordie Shore* star has decided that we haven't seen enough of her antics on the reality show, and has taken to vlogging. Her crazy personality is certainly infectious, although she does have a habit of over-sharing! Her ex-boyfriend, Gary Beadle, also made a few videos on his own channel, but his interest was short-lived.

Karlie Kloss

Taylor Swift's supermodel best friend started her YouTube channel in 2015, and since then she has been treating us to regular updates of what it is like to be a world famous fashion icon. Proving that she has a brain by taking us along on her coding journey, and showing us all that models really do eat by baking cookies, life is one big adventure for Karlie.

When Vloggers Unite

Some YouTubers collaborate so often that they should really combine their accounts, while others prefer to invite guests onto their blogs just once in a while. Of course, vlogger couples regularly gatecrash each other's videos. One thing is for sure though, we love it when we get two vloggers for the price of one. Here are some of our favourite combinations.

Amazing Phil — Caspar Lee

Jim Chapman — Marcus Butler

Marcus Butler — Pointless Blog

Smosh — Lee Newton

Pointless Blog — Roman Atwood

Joe Sugg — Joey Graceffa

Grace Helbig — Joe Sugg

Zoella — SacconeJolys

Sprinkle of Glitter — Zoella

Obviously, there are far more, but these stood out for us. Who knows what amazing collaborations will happen in the coming year!

Music to Our Ears

While the content that is included in the vlogs is usually interesting and fun, sometimes the background music can be a little bit... questionable! Due to usage rights and copyright laws, vloggers cannot just play the latest chart music as they would be liable to a hefty fine. And although it is possible to license any song they wish to use, with the correct permissions, for most this is expensive and time consuming (and wouldn't make for a very exciting video blog). It would also mean they would have to wait to upload the video they wanted to use it on.

If any YouTuber were to use a song without usage rights, their account would be deleted, and the person who owns the master rights to the song could pursue legal action.

So, what's a YouTuber to do? Luckily, the video streaming website has come up with an audio gallery of free-to-use music, so that no vlog has to be empty of background tunes. If you are a wannabe vlogger just starting out, make sure you familiarise yourself with this process, since it will help add an extra layer of appeal to your videos.

Here's how YouTube Audio works:

1. Log into your account.

2. Go to the Creator Studio menu.

3. Click on the Create dropdown on the left hand side menu, where you will find the Audio Library. Click on this.

4. Here you will find a long, long list of free music and sound effects for use on your vlog. Some of them will come with usage instructions that must be followed if you wish to use them, or you will still run the risk of legal proceedings. This is usually just a sentence or so that should be added to the vlog description, crediting the source of the song.

There are some songs that seem to pop up again and again. These include *How's it Going* by Martin Felix Kaczmarski, *Silent Partner* by Parasail and *Venice Beach* by Topher Mohr and Alex Elena. See if you can find them in the audio gallery and then keep an eye out for them in some of the more popular vlogs. We promise they will pop up a lot!

One of the key things these songs have in common is that they tend to be upbeat and happy, since the vlogger's role is to entertain, and so they are usually brimming with enthusiasm themselves. If they ever do have to make a more sombre blog, they would usually choose to leave out music altogether, rather than play a sad song, as this can make the video feel false and forced.

Alternatively, if music is your talent, play your own music on your vlog. It could be your path to fame and fortune!

Best Fashion Moments in Vlogging

These guys spend their lives in front of the camera, so looking good is essential. Here are some of our favourite fashion moments:

Bethany Mota looks super classy at the Kids Choice Awards in this stylish jumpsuit with subtle cut outs by Jay Godfrey.

How cute does Grace Helbig look here? Showing the world how to wear lilac in an Elizabeth and James minidress, complete with a Kate Spade ice cream clutch. Super-sweet!

Wow! Tanya Burr was dressed to impress at the British Fashion Awards in 2015. Oozing body confidence, this outfit by Barbara Casasola looked amazing, and of course, her make-up was perfect.

Woah, Lilly Singh is one super-tough rock chic you don't want to mess with! Seriously though, this outfit is fierce, and Lilly pulls it off effortlessly. Her body suit is by YBNB and skirt by Ground Zero Official.

Niomi Smart nails the nautical look at the very.co.uk Can't Wait For Summer Pool Party. Ahoy Sailor!

Puzzles

Have you read your Annual from cover to cover? Time to test your knowledge!

Crossword

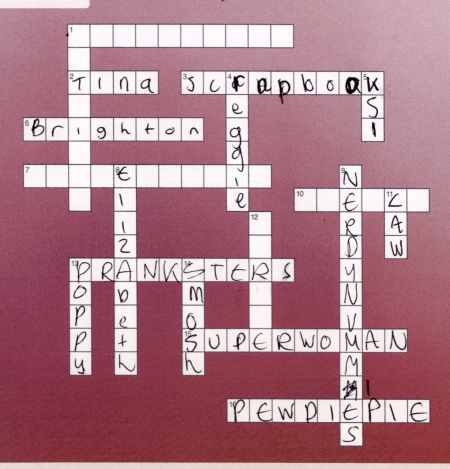

Across

1. The first ever video on YouTube. (2,2,3,3)
2. Lilly Singh's older sister. (4)
3. Alfie Deyes' 2016 book, 'The _____ of My Life'. (9)
6. Seaside town that Alfie Deyes and Zoella call home. (8)
7. This vlogger is a former semi-finalist of the Miss New Jersey beauty pageant. (5,6)
10. Pippin and Percy's owner. (6)
13. 'Natural Born _____', feature film released by Roman Atwood and his vlogger peers in 2016. (10)
15. Lilly Singh's alter-ego. (10)
16. Gamer Felix Kjellberg's vlogging name. (9)

Down

1. Rhett & Link's second channel, 'Good _____ Morning'. (8)
4. Essie Button's four-legged friend. (6)
5. Vlogger with Guinness World Record for Most Goals Scored Against a Computer. (3)
8. Zoe Sugg's middle name. (9)
9. Rosanna Pansino's tasty YouTube series. (5,7)
11. Degree Danisonfire was studying before he took up vlogging. (3)
12. Michelle Phan's most popular video, '_____ Transformation'. (6)
13. Alfie's aspiring sister, _____ Deyes. (5)
14. Comedy duo Ian Andrew Hecox and Anthony Padilla. (5)

Answers on page 61.

Wordsearch

Find the words in the grid. Words can go horizontally, vertically and diagonally in all eight directions.

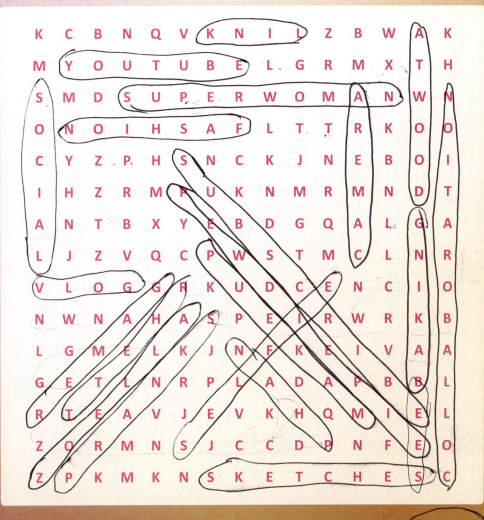

Atwood Baking Selfie Pranks
Camera Collaboration Sketches Social
Fashion Gamer Subscribe Rhett
Link Makeup Superwoman Youtube
Pewdiepie Phan Vlog Zoella

Answers on page 61.

Answers

**Page 12:
Vlogging Quiz**
1. c.
2. b.
3. a.
4. b.
5. a.
6. d.
7. d.
8. c.

**Page 26:
True or False?**
1. True
2. False
3. True
4. True
5. False

**Page 26:
Anagrams**
1. Marcus Butler
2. Casper Lee
3. Alfie Deyes
4. Louise Pentland
5. Joe Sugg
6. Dan Howell
7. Tanya Burr
8. Bethany Mota

Page 26: Which YouTuber are you?
Mostly As: Rosanna Pansino   Mostly Bs: Roman Atwood
Mostly Cs: StampyLongNose   Mostly Ds: Tanya Burr

Page 27: Spot the Difference

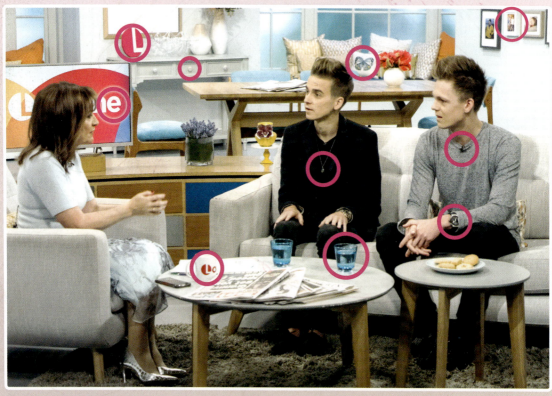

Page 58: Crossword

Page 59: Wordsearch